HISTORY
FOR
PEACE
TRACTS

How do we understand what was, grapple with
what is and prepare for what is likely to be,
as a nation, as a people, as a community,
as individuals?

This series is an attempt to address this question
by putting into print thoughts, ideas and
concerns of some of South Asia's most
seminal thinkers.

*In memory of Kozo Yamamura (1934–2017)*

# Thinking Aloud

JERRY PINTO

LONDON NEW YORK CALCUTTA

The texts in this volume are updated editions of lectures delivered at History for Peace conferences in 2017, 2018 and 2022.

Visit historyforpeace.pw to read similar resources.

**Seagull Books, 2025**

© Jerry Pinto, 2025

First published in volume form
by Seagull Books, 2025

ISBN 978 1 80309 478 6

**British Library Cataloguing-in-Publication Data**

A catalogue record for this book
is available from the British Library

Typeset by Seagull Books, Calcutta, India

Printed and bound by WordsWorth India,
New Delhi, India

# CONTENTS

# BOLLYWOOD AND THE IDEA OF THE NATION

If you should wish to snarl when someone suggests that Bollywood is a national cinema, I shall be happy to provide bass notes. I do not think linguistic chauvinism is a good thing in India. I once asked Professor Ganesh N. Devy, who had just finished work on the monumental Linguistic Survey of India, how many languages we had. He said: 'One thousand five hundred, and we're still counting.' No single language's cinema can hope to provide a national cinema in India; there are other cinemas that make more money, there are other cinemas which have a higher viewership, there are other cinemas that have certainly done much more to push the bounds of cinema, to refine its language, to challenge its suppositions and to refine its grammar. But Bollywood is the cinema I know, and I suspect it may be a cinema we are all familiar with, whatever our home language, heart language or state language. Therefore, perhaps it is meet to consider what role it has had in the building of the nation, in moments when it consciously chose to do so; as also when it contributed to the project by simply being a form of mass media, thus adding to our sense of who we are and who we might like to be.

Rewind to 1943. *Kismet*, directed by Gyan Mukherjee and starring Ashok

Kumar and Mumtaz Shanti was released. The big song in it was '*Door hato eh duniyawalon, Hindustan hamaara hai*' (Go away, people of the world, Hindustan is ours). How did the British censor allow it? Because the producer and director argued that while the Second World War was raging, the message was directed at the Axis powers: 'We are saying this to Japan. We are saying this to Germany. They will come and attack us. We don't want them here.'

It is a moment of strategic duplicity and one we celebrate today. But I think it is wise to look at the lyrics of the song.

> *Aaj Himaalaya ki choti se*
> *    humne phir lalkaaraa hai—*
> *Door hato eh duniyaawalon,*
> *    Hindustan hamaara hai.*

From the heights of
    the Himalaya, we declare—
Go away, people of the world,
    Hindustan is ours.

All this as young soldiers beat drums and
perform a marchpast on a stage.

*Jahaan hamaara Taj Mahal hai*
    *aur Qutb Minaaraa hai,*
*Jahaan hamaare mandir-masjid,*
    *Sikhon ka gurdwara hai,*
*Is dharti par kadam badhaana,*
    *atyaachaar tumhaara hai.*

Here you'll find the Taj Mahal
    and the mighty Qutb Minara
Here, the temple, the mosque
    and the Sikh gurudwara,
Stepping on to this land would be
    an atrocity on your part.

Kavi Pradeep probably wrote these lines knowing that no one would argue with them. No one could possibly have argued with them in 1943. I am not implying that there was a prelapsarian, pre-Partition past; I am talking instead about the assumptions made by the nationalist movement.

> *Shuru huaa hai jung tumhaara,*
> *jaag utho Hindustaani.*
> *Tum na kisi ke aage jhuknaa,*
> *German ho ya Jaapaani.*
> *Aaj sabhi ke liye hamaara*
> *yahi qaumi naaraa hai*:
> *Door hato . . .*

> Rise and wake, Hindustani,
> the war has been declared.
> Do not bend the knee before
> any German or Japanese.

Today the call goes out from
     all our communities:
Stay away . . .

Now things become a little clearer, I
hope, and the British censors' decision to
leave the song alone more
understandable. *German ho ya Jaapaani*
can be a synecdoche, a part for the
whole, but the lines are there and what
we were told about Kavi Pradeep writing
from the heart may have to be revised a
little.

But *Kismet* is as good a starting point
as any. I can do no more here than pick
films that I have seen and remember. And
so, I should like to cut to *Mother India*
(directed by Mehboob Khan, 1957) and
make two quick points.

At this point in time, the nation is
equated with motherhood. If the

hallmark of the good mother was her willingness to suffer, then the motherland was also marked by suffering. And it is within this context that we see Radha (played by Nargis) pulling the plough because her husband has abandoned her after the loss of both his arms in an agricultural accident and walked away into India. The ploughing cattle are dead too. Now she must pull the plough herself, she must suffer to make the earth bring forth a new crop. Behind her, her two sons scramble to sow the seed.

Radha sings in the voice of Lata Mangeshkar:

*Duniya mein hum aaye hain,*
    *toh jeena hi padegaa,*
*Jeevan hai agar zeher,*
    *toh peena hi padega.*

> Now that we have come into this
> > world, we must live.
> If life is poison, we must
> > drain the cup.

This was the image that was carried on all the posters whenever the film was shown in theatres across Bombay (as it was then known) as matinee shows (as they were then known) through the 1980s. Iconographically, the image of Radha leaning a weary head on the plough always brought to my mind the image of Christ dragging his cross along the Via Dolorosa, en route to the crucifixion. Or was this only the result of my Roman Catholic upbringing?

The title tells you something of the zeitgeist. If Radha is Mother India, then the nation is defined as a woman. In the beginning of the film, Radha pays her respects to the earth as tractors rumble past her. The titles run on a montage of images that pays homage to the Nehruvian idea of India: bridges, cranes, tractors, excavators, electricity lines . . . all these point to the nation the Mother has birthed.

And where did that come from? It came from suffering and sacrifice. Radha would eventually take up her gun—but only to defend a woman's honour. She would kill her own son—and this blood sacrifice would bring the new India to birth.

Yes, a woman. Her achievements are defined in terms of her survival. Her greatest achievement, for which she is shown to be honoured at the beginning of the film, is that she could give up her beloved son in the interests of dharma.

In the 1950s, Bollywood is said to have had its Golden Age. We call it this because we cherry-pick the films made by a handful of filmmakers who were invested in constructing a particular vision of the nation. They would invite Gandhi to watch their films (a hopeless cause; the Mahatma would have nothing to do with cinema); they would organize special screenings for Nehru; and if he wrote them a letter, it would go into their publicity material.

There is a sinusoidal curve that Bollywood follows—good decade and bad decade. In the 1950s, *Pyaasa* (directed by Guru Dutt, 1957) would have a hero like Vijay (played by Dutt himself)—an unemployed poet and thus a social outcaste—who would reject the false values of a materialist–capitalist society. He would have nothing to do with *yeh mehelon, yeh taqton yeh tajon ki duniya* (this world of palaces, thrones, crowns). Once again, the iconography of Christian suffering is represented when Vijay throws open the doors of the auditorium where his poetry is being celebrated after his supposed death. There he stands, his arms thrown out, a poor forked thing, and once again, we see Christ, now on the cross.

In the 1960s, the hero didn't care if the world called him uncouth or a *Junglee* (directed by Subodh Mukherjee, 1961). Masculinity was represented by a burst of pubescence, all made of cotton candy and fluff. Biswajit and Rajendra Kapoor arrived with lipstick for men (and I have never seen such luminous lips in my life.) The nation is now unimportant; it can be made and unmade in other places.

Then the 1970s, a time of strife, turmoil and terror. The angry young man has routinely been examined as a critique of the nation-state, as a response to the collapse of the dream of an equitable society, as a response to the end of a (to my mind, somewhat mythic) belief that Utopia was around the corner. It is interesting, then, to compare the Vijay of *Trishul* (directed by Yash Chopra, 1978) with the Devdas of *Devdas* (directed by Bimal Roy, 1955). The eponymous hero (played by Dilip Kumar) is crushed by his father and the weight of tradition whereas Vijay (played by Amitabh Bachchan) defeats his father (played by Sanjeev Kumar) and crushes him—Oedipus Rex comes to Bollywood for the first time, although with a refinement. The original Oedipus had no idea that he was killing Laius. Vijay knows; his knowledge fuels his rage. He wants to destroy his father and he does so, taking his secretary, then his company and finally his family. We recognize here the value of history, we recognize, at last, the synthesis that follows thesis and antithesis. We recognize the value of rebellion. Flying fists will do what sighs could not. For Devdas never got his lady love, nor could he accept the love that was offered, not until Anurag Kashyap made *Dev.D* (2009) and Dev (played by Abhay Deol) dragged his sorry self back to the new Leni / Chanda / Chandramukhi (played by Kalki Koechlin) to ask for a second chance at love.

But both Kumar's Devdas and Bachchan's Vijay are men. The nation is now a man. The nation must choose. Standing for the nation, the hero can die at the end and become immortal; or he can fight and win in battle. These men—Devdas and Vijay—represent different ends of the spectrum. Their names tell you a story. One is the servitor of the Gods, the other is victory sought through the body in the service of rage.

The 1980s were a terrible time, aesthetically. We did have a couple of interesting films: *Mashaal* (Yash Chopra, 1984) and surprise hits from the art house: *Jaane Bhi Do Yaaro* (Kundan Shah, 1983), *Saaransh* (Mahesh Bhatt, 1984) and *Ardh Satya* (Govind Nihalani, 1983). But, for the most part, the 1980s meant bad music, aerobic-style dancing and formulaic plots repeated ad nauseam.

Yet, each repetition has its value in formulating the state. When young people die for their love, as they did in *Qayamat Se Qayamat Tak* (Mansoor Khan, 1988), what had shifted since the producers of *Bobby* (directed by Raj Kapoor, 1977) insisted on a happy ending with the lovers reunited, the Hindu boy rescued by the Christian father, the Christian girl rescued by the Hindu father? Was it only the success of *Ek Duuje Ke Liye* (directed by K. Balachander, 1981), in which the lovers die in the end, a film that went on to become the box office smash of the year? Why is it that double death came to mean box office success, from *Qayamat se Qayamat Tak* (directed by Mansoor Khan, 1988) right up to *Ishaqzaade* (directed by Habib Faisal, 2012)?

*

Let me take a step back in time. We looked at *Mother India* in 1957, the same year that B. R. Chopra made *Naya Daur*, a film which could be seen as pitching the Gandhian model of the Indian village against the Nehruvian vision of India. Let us now consider a film released three years later: *Mughal-e-Azam* (directed by K. Asif, 1960). After we have been warned by a panel that reads 'History and legend link the story of our past. When both are fused in the crucible of art and imagination, the spirit of this great land is revealed in all its splendour and beauty,' the opening sequence has what we would call a 'physical map' rising over a toyland of monuments and buildings. The man begins speaking to us in a man's voice. This is interesting because much of the imagery comes from the idea of a woman, a passive woman who has admirers, who can be enchained and freed, who can be looted or adorned. This representation of the nation says:

*Main Hindostan hoon. Himalaya meri sarhadon ka nigehbaan hai; Ganga meri pavitrata ki saugandh. Taareeq-e ibtada se, main andheron aur ujaalon ka saathi hoon aur mere khaak par sang-e marmar ke chaadaron mein lipti hui yeh imaaratein duniya ko keh rahi hai ki zaalimon ne mujhe loota aur meherbaanon ne mujhe savaaraa, naadaanon ne mujhe zanjeerein pehna di aur mere chaahanewaalon ne unhein kaat pheka. Mere in chaahanewaalon ek insaan ka naam Jalal-ud-din Muhammad Akbar tha. Akbar ne mujhse pyaar kiya. Mazhab aur rasm-rivaayat ke deewaaron se buland hokar insaan ko insaan se mohabbat karna sikhaaya aur mujhe hamesha ke liye seene se lagaa liya . . .*

The glory of those lines lies in their ornamental, courtly Urdu but I shall attempt a translation:

I am Hindostan. The Himalaya stands as my guardian; the River Ganges a witness to my purity. From the beginning of time, I have walked with the shadows and bathed in the light, and these buildings that stand in ashes, swathed in sheaths of marble, are witness to the fact that tyrants

have looted me and my beloveds
have adorned me, that the naive
bound me in chains, but my lovers
shattered my fetters and set me
free. One of my lovers was a man
called Jalal-ud-din Muhammad
Akbar. Akbar loved me.
Transcending the barriers of caste
and creed, he taught people to
love each other and he took me
for his own and forever . . .

I could spend hours breaking this down.
As opposed to the manmade Taj Mahal
and Qutb Minar, here the marks of the
nation are natural, even though this is not
the shape of the Mughal Empire.
Establishing Akbar as a great king is
important, of course, but what is more
important is his secularism, which is
highlighted by talking about how he

transcends religion and teaches all men to love.

I shall leave the rest for you to decode as you watch the film and enjoy the sneeze-and-you-miss-it scene in which, on the occasion of Janmashtami, the emperor rocks a cradle in which a small statue of Bal Krishna sits. Note the sacrifice of Durjan the Rajput (played by Ajit), friend to Prince Salim, and the great conclusion in which the honour of the Mughals is upheld by a woman's sacrifice of her love. The Oedipal conflict that love is visited upon the family—and since this is a royal family, consequently upon the state—is averted by the power of her sacrifice.

Yes, a woman.

Yes, a sacrifice.

*

If I may be allowed a parenthetical remark here: even though the woman has been held to be central to the making of the nation-state, I don't think most Indian men know how to converse with a woman who is not their mother or sister. The home is safe ground. The women to be found there are facts of life. But then hormones hit, and suddenly they are out in the world, surrounded by women they would love to talk to—only they don't know how. What kind of state can we devise if half of it has no way of communicating with the other half? We have an economy of information that is conservative in the first place. Now add to this the fact that young male India has no models for ordinary conversation.

Their models are '*Aati kya Khandala*?' (literally: Come with me to

Khandala? Figuratively: How about a dirty weekend with me?) and '*Hasee toh phasee*' (If she smiles, she's hooked.) That a woman might have interests and ideas and opinions and these might be explored as routes to friendship are never allowed for in Bollywood.

In Bollywood, a 'no' from a woman must be construed as a prelude to a 'yes'. The assumption is that the woman is eternally coy and unable to face her own sexual desires. Therefore, it is up to the man to, literally, force the issue. For the longest time, what was romance? Romance was Urdu shayari based on the assumption that the beloved is with the rival and tormenting you, and that out of this torment will suddenly bloom the *gulistan* (the garden) of your heart, fertilized by the great sorrows of your love.

Let me take you back to the character of Devdas again. There must be a reason why we have returned to him again and again, remade the film in so many languages and for so many generations. But what sort of a model is he? Here is a man unable to achieve adulthood. In the shortcuts of cinema, this is generally shown as an Oedipal rebellion. Devdas cannot revolt against his father, and therefore against the patriarchy and the strictures and structures of society; he ends up tongue tied. He cannot speak his love, so he hits his beloved. He cannot love a woman who offers him love and instead rejects her; there is no suggestion in any of the films I have seen that this is because Chandramukhi is a sex worker. But we should bear in mind that he is a privileged upper-caste, upper-class man of the nineteenth century and would therefore have the biases of his kind.

After that, we needed a dramatic, definitive, masculinist presence. In the 1970s, another prototype of brokenness is released on to the world: the Oedipally fixated Vijay, played by Amitabh Bachchan. In this version of Oedipus, the struggle was always over the figure of the mother: whether it was in *Deewaar* (directed by Yash Chopra, 1975) or *Shakti* (directed by Ramesh Sippy, 1982). The woman is now decorative. She will try to seduce the hero, she will be fascinated by his lone-wolf aura. All you have to do is read the Brontë sisters to see where that came from—Rochester is the paradigm. He even allows Jane to heal him. He is delightful even if—or perhaps because—he is toxic.

He smoulders but it is all mind, no body, up to this point. Look at the shape of the Indian hero. Imagine taking off Raj Kapoor's shirt and seeing his six pack. Imagine Shammi Kapoor bare-chested, or Dev Anand. Or consider Shah Rukh from the 1990s. He gave off an easy sensuality, but it was a suggestion in his movements, in his eyes, in his intensity. It was not his body on which he relied.

This has changed and so has Shah Rukh, whose shirt now flies off his newly gym-toned body. Now every struggler has a six-pack. This is the new masculinity. Anuradha Kapoor's essay on the depictions of Ram sheds some light on this.[1] She describes how the Ram of Raja Ravi Verma is markedly different from the martial and muscular Ram of the first Hindutva posters—*Kasam Ram ki khaate hai, hum mandir wahin banaenge* (We swear by Lord Ram, we will build the temple right there). Now, Ram suddenly has the V-shaped body of Arnold Schwarzenegger.

How do you become a man? In the old days, you killed an animal and they smeared its blood on your face. Hrithik Roshan becomes a man by picking up a gun. This is the trajectory we follow, determined by the phallocracy of the patriarchy. We gain cinematic testosterone and lose our conscience.

End of parenthetical remarks.

*

I would like now to turn to *Amar Akbar Anthony* (1977), one of the greatest Bollywood films ever made by one of the auteurs of Indian cinema, Manmohan Desai. Even attempting to recount its plot leaves you tangled in confusion. This is why it is such pure cinema. It refuses reduction and conversion to words. I saw it when I was eleven years old, and though I had then but a poor penn'orth of Hindi, I got every twist and turn in the plot. I remember delighting in every reel, every completely magnificent moment. I followed it without effort.

For those lucky enough not to have seen AAA (as we called it)—lucky because you can now watch it and witness its blackswanness—here's my attempt at retelling the story in the wrong medium:

A terrible rich man kills someone by mistake; he asks his loyal driver, Kishanlal, to take the blame and promises that he will look after the driver's family and his three children. Kishanlal takes the fall, goes to jail but when he comes out, he finds his wife is dying of tuberculosis and his sons are starving. His boss has reneged on the deal. He goes to confront his boss, and in return for his loyalty, his boss orders his henchmen to kill Kishanlal. He eludes them and jumps into a car full of gold bullion and comes home to find his wife has gone off to commit suicide. He picks up his children, but the goons are still in hot pursuit, so he stashes the children for safety in a nearby park, in the shadow of a statue of Mahatma Gandhi, and continues to take evasive action. His eldest son runs after the car but is knocked down and left by the side of the road. A policeman takes the boy home, adopts him and names him Amar. The second boy is adopted by a Muslim tailor and named Akbar. The third child falls asleep in front of a Christian church and is adopted by the priests; he is Anthony. When Kishenlal returns, his sons are gone. The boys grow up in their adoptive homes.

One day, they are called to a hospital to give blood to a woman who is ill. They do not know it but they are donating blood to their mother.

Now, everyone is familiar with the routine of donating blood: you squeeze a stress ball, avert your eyes until a capacious baggy of blood is drawn, which is then whisked off to the blood bank. There it joins other anonymous bottles of blood, ready to revive those in need. But in Manmohan Desai's magnificent, corny spectacle, this banality is not allowed to get in the way. The three young men are seen lying in a hospital ward, and each declares his name as a nurse hooks him up to a single blood donation line:

'Amar,' declares the Hindu as his blood rises up, against the laws of gravity, and flows towards the blood on the next bed.

'Akbar,' declares the Muslim, and his blood rises up to join Amar's blood and flows towards the third line and the third bed where

'Anthony,' declares the Christian. The three bloodstreams, conjoined, flow down into the arm of the old woman who they do not know is their mother. (But we know. This is delicious knowledge.)

The playback song underlined what was happening, asking:

*Kya iski keemat chukaani nahin?*
*Khoon khoon hota hai paani*
    *nahin.*

Must one not pay one's debt?
For this is blood, not water.

The man next to me began to weep and I discovered that I was weeping too. We wept together.

Later, Manmohan Desai was told that this was not the way blood was donated. He responded that he was not making a documentary, he was making a film. And this was not about encouraging blood donation; it was about suggesting a way

in which a nation is to be constructed,
out of bits and parts. You do not get a
nation unless Amar, Akbar and Anthony
come together, offering blood and blood
and blood, paying their debt to the
motherland. There is so much at work
here. The notion of purity is disrupted as
three bloodstreams head upstream and
home. The audience knows all along that
all three boys were born into a Hindu
family, though they now practise
different faiths. We see them at this.
Anthony is shown in church in several
scenes, once confessing to the old priest
who adopted him, once as a server at the
altar on Easter Sunday. (Has there ever
been an Easter Sunday like that one with
tie and tails and top-hat and a rotating
Easter egg that can hold a six-foot man?)
Akbar sings a qawwali of devotion to Sai

Baba of Shirdi: a man whose followers came from every faith, a man who simply insisted that '*Sabka maalik ek*'. (There is but one master.) We do not see Amar offering worship as a Hindu but he had grown up to be a police inspector, representing the state.

All this is tied up to Mother India, in the form of a blind woman, the mother of the three young men, a mother whose sight will be returned to her at the end of the qawwali and who will be defended by a snake.

But the narrative was changing. Now the nation would be built by men and would be defined by men. If you look at *Border* (directed by J. P. Dutta, 1997) or *LOC: Kargil* (directed by J. P. Dutta, 2003) or *Gadar: Ek Prem Katha* (directed by Anil Sharma, 2001), you will

see that Bollywood has now decided it is
men who make history while women
simply sit at home and wait for news
from the frontier. But there is no trace of
the soul-searching of *Haqeeqat* (directed
by Chetan Anand, 1964) or of *Hum
Dono* (directed by Vijay Anand, 1961)
where an army officer can suddenly riff
on war:

> *Woh kaunsi taaqat hai, Captain,
> jo hume apne gharon se, apne
> pyaar se, apne maa-baap se,
> door-door laakar kandhon pe
> bandookein rakhne ko majboor
> kar deti hai? Haalaaki hum jaante
> hain ki jung buri hai, hinsa buri
> hai, nafrat buri hai, pet ki aag ya
> shaurat ki bhook ya desh ka
> pyaar? Ya hamaari insaaniyat jo
> haiwaaniyat ke khilaaf bhadak*

*utathi hai? Insaan ke andar ka*
*loha apni chamak dikhaane ke*
*liye mauqe ki taat mein rehta hai*
*aur jab mauqaa aataa hai to woh*
*yeh nahin dekhta ki uski biwi ka*
*dil toottha hai, ya uski maa ka dil*
*toottha hai, ya uski premika ka*
*dil toottha hai . . .*

What force is this, Captain, that
drags us from our homes, our
loves, our parents and brings us
here, puts guns to our shoulders?
When we know that war is
wrong, that violence is wrong,
that hatred is wrong, is it hunger
or hunger for fame or the love of
one's country? Or is it our
humanity that revolts against
beastliness in others? A man
waits for the opportunity to show

his mettle and when that
opportunity arises, he does not
consider whether his mother's
heart will break or his wife's
heart or his lover's . . .

But even these seem innocent compared
with the nation-building attempts of *The
Kashmir Files* (Vivek Agnihotri, 2022)
and *The Kerala Story* (Sudipto Sen,
2023). If you would like to see the
modern reinvention of reality, look no
further than *Gadar 2* (Anil Sharma,
2023) where the protagonist announces
that the Indian Muslim is so happy that
if Pakistan were to open its borders, it
would end up half empty.

*

In the 1950s, a filmmaker like Raj Kapoor and a writer like Khwaja Ahmad Abbas sat in the same room and planned the films they would make under the banner R. K. Films. Kapoor was the showman and Abbas his political and social conscience. When Abbas branched out to make his own films, Kapoor's downslide began, leading us to *Ram Teri Ganga Maili* (1985).

Many progressive writers (read socialist or leftist) were active in Bombay during this period. 'I could live on my writing for cinema,' writes Ismat Chughtai in her memoir *Kaghazi hai Pairahan* (1988). Chughtai, Kaifi Azmi and Sahir Ludhianvi, all inhabited the same city. And films like *Haqeeqat* are a product of that symbiotic environment.

But by the time of *Border* and *LOC*, the split is total. The progressives and leftists had all moved on. Like Shyam Benegal, they immersed themselves in the art-house movement, happy as larks. Now they didn't have to deal with demands like '*Ek mujra* sequence *ke liye ek gaana de do, yaar*' (Give me a song for a mujra sequence, buddy). But their cinema was also drifting away from the people.

*

I had a poignant encounter with an independent filmmaker, who shall go unnamed. We were travelling together when he asked me about my destination. I said that I was heading to a conference in London on Bollywood. He sighed and reflected on how, in his time, filmmakers were either *bhakts* (devotees) of Saraswati or Lakshmi. He, and his kind, made films for Saraswati, for art, while commercial filmmakers created theirs for Lakshmi, for money. Saraswati rewarded his kind with critical attention; Lakshmi rewarded the other with wealth. And having said this, he was very puzzled by the critical attention that classical Bollywood was then receiving.

He was not wrong. Something had changed.

At one of the first international screenings of *Amar Akbar Anthony*, presented by Rosie Thomas and Behroze Gandhy, at an Italian film festival, the audience responded with a slow clap: the Italian way of saying, 'Go home, this is not what we want to listen to.'

Cut to 2012 and we are having conferences on 'the soft power of Bollywood'! In Abu Dhabi! Business class tickets for everyone! No need for a visa—the embassy men will escort you from the airport to your hotel!

What changed? Globalization. And liberalization. Up to that point, the dominant narrative about India was one of heart-stopping despair. It was about disease, open defecation, corruption and the failure of the state to provide basic amenities to its people.

In 1992–93, the world suddenly discovered that we were a market. (I remember interviewing a vice-president of Lee Jeans when they launched in India. 'I want babies to be in Lee diapers,' he said. And with a straight face. I wondered whether he was serious. He certainly looked it. He even gave me the headline I wanted: 'Lee VP sees Indian babies in denim diapers'. I knew he was feeding it to me. Once India was recognized as a market, we were allowed to take pride in ourselves—because they were proud of us.)

*

As a teacher myself, I know we like to believe we make a lasting impact on our students, hoping they will remember what we have taught them. Yet, if I were to ask a history teacher what the cosine of an angle is, or the value of $(a + b)$ raised to the power of three, s/he/they might be at a loss. It's no more surprising to forget a binomial expansion than to forget who Tipu Sultan was. A history teacher may have a greater investment in ensuring students remember Tipu Sultan—but mathematics is a modality of engagement with logic—if that slips you by, then logic slips you by. Up to a certain point, the only exposure to logic many people have is through mathematics, even if it is taught without explicit reference to logic itself. So how can you insist that others remember their history—while excusing yourself for forgetting your chemistry or mathematics? Are we guilty of prioritizing certain forms of knowledge simply because they are of more value to us? Perhaps we do it unknowingly, but the message is clear: they should know their history, but I can forget my botany.

And if our system is a failure, then let us assume that most young people have information sources beyond the classroom, that everything they think they know about our history does not come from our textbooks. Those textbooks have left no impact. But we are humans—we want to know who we are, we want to know the story of our tribe. The most trivial form of this desire for tribal knowledge is gossip; its most noble forms are literature and history. Deprived of a healthy connection with both these because of unimaginative teaching, colonial syllabi, examinations that focus of rote learning and a complete delinking of these two subjects from each other and from life, something else fills the gaps. Many thinkers have reminded us that nationalism is shallow. We know we should not care for shallow, but the truth is that we love what is shallow. Shallow is easy, shallow makes no great demands on us. And Hindi cinema, Bollywood, being perennially, perpetually, unashamedly shallow, presents us with the ideal formulation for understanding the nation-state.

But what's terrifying is that history is being reconstructed and revised by the Twitterati and in editing studios where soundtracks are overlaid on recorded events. This distorted reality is then widely circulated. And since we are now in a space where we only hear and believe what we want to hear and believe, the correctives are ignored. How will the teacher of history respond? How will the makers of history respond to a world of deep fakes, artificial intelligence and the democratization of the processes by which history is made? What will we do when the power is taken from us?

As journalists, we were aware of our role in making history. If Matthew Arnold is believed to have said that journalism is literature in a hurry, Thomas Griffiths called journalism literature on the run. Philip L. Graham, the president and publisher of *The Washington Post* is supposed to have said that journalism is the first rough draft of history. History used to be made in the newspapers. Even in ordinary conversation, we quoted our sources: 'I read it in the newspapers.' Then, it shifted to 'I saw it on television'. This was a witnessing, and our role as witness made it even more believable even if we saw only what the cameraman pointed his camera at, what footage the editor chose, what stories the monolithic corporation, whether funded by the state or private capital, decided we should see.

The large corporations that Noam Chomsky warned us about were worried about their credibility. They wanted to be recognized as purveyors of reliable and factual news. Part of this was the realpolitik of capitalism, part of it was the awareness that there were laws of libel and that they could be sued. But what about the troll who puts out a video that goes viral? 'I saw it on Twitter,' say his followers, and the result is that history is made by those who have a desire to represent not what happened but what they want to say has happened. They know they are biased. In fact, they are proud of these biases. And they are prouder still of introducing these biases into their work.

That suggests something even more widespread. It suggests a shift of values, a shift in how we judge ourselves. If we no longer accept objectivity as a goal, then how do we judge what we read? If we are not objective here, how do others judge us?

The seductions of Bollywood were always devised to snatch us away from our quotidian analysis of who we are. Is this the problem? The problem is not with our circumstances. Our circumstances have always been bad, in every decade of the last few centuries, any number of editorials would tell you that we are on the verge of the apocalypse. If you read nineteenth-century journalism or eighteenth-century social critiques, you notice the same narratives emerge again and again: the rich have gotten richer, the poor poorer. The young have never been so shallow, the old never so tired.

It's been nearly a hundred years since that beast was slouching towards Bethlehem in Yeats' poem. And we have seen some pretty good beasts come down the pike.

We are all agreed that the making of a nation's history, the making of a nation's story is fundamental to its notion of itself and how that self will play out in its attitudes to the weakest sections of its self. Now imagine the role Bollywood plays in all this. None! There is no room for something so shallow, so lightheaded, so ignorant in a discussion of the making of history. How could there be? History begins with *jigyaasa*, the desire to know. Bollywood has rarely, if ever, wanted to know—it is deliberately ignorant, it is often dangerously naive.

But the moral universe of Hindi cinema mirrors the moral outlook of our students. A teacher said that her one of her students asked her whether Tipu Sultan was a good guy or a bad guy. In other words, the student could well have been asking: Is he Gabbar Singh, the villain of *Sholay*, or is he the Thakur, the prime mover of the plot and the axis of the moral sphere?

The student was speaking in dichotomies; he had been taught to do so by popular cinema and populist fiction too. These are the binaries in which our children have been schooled. In this world, the good guys beat the bad guys and the moral universe is set right again. They want Tipu Sultan or Nehru or Gandhi or whoever is being talked about to fit into a Venn diagram in which there are good guys and bad guys with no intersection set, into a polarized world whose morality is so simple as to be immoral.

What we are contending with is not just the naivete of the young person, coming to a teacher and asking for a judgement they should know they ought not to make but which they feel empowered to make. The problem may be that we do not teach philosophy in our schools and it is an optional subject in college so few students think about thinking.

History strives for consensus. The historian tries to establish the facts and extrapolate from those facts. And yet research continues—new archives are discovered and new inscriptions uncovered, and over time, the facts begin to rearrange themselves. This is the magic of research, and the greatest of historians—like the greatest of scientists—must be willing to acknowledge that facts mutate as our knowledge grows and our technology improves.

We all know that there is never a single narrative. Consider the last time a couple you know went through a divorce. If you were close to both, it is likely that you will hear two versions of the same marriage. It may seem as if you are hearing two different stories here. Perhaps you like the wife more than you like the husband. Perhaps she is the friend you have known for many years before she married. You might be tempted, therefore, to privilege her account over his. But that is bias. It is a crude, ahistorical reaction that emerges from the crucible of our loves and our hates, our loyalties and prejudices. We know we cannot trust this instinct, but how we want to!

So we return to those two differing stories. Is one right and the other wrong? Are there elements of truth in both stories? What prisms have been interposed between us and what actually happened? The prism of positionality within the relationship—husband vs wife; the prism of time—memory is not infallible; the prism of positionality outside the relationship—whose friend are you? Is there room, then, for contending versions? How can there be? We have been taught to believe in unitary truths.

But when we take this to the macro-level, what room does that leave for the versions written by the vanquished? How do we account for the colonial narrative and the narratives of the colonized? How do we account for the view from the boat being very different from the view from the shore?[2] What room does a unitary narrative leave for Adivasi, Dalit and tribal histories? What room does that leave for women's perspectives of history? How do we accommodate the subaltern? And if we can make room for all these, should we also find a way to accommodate the right-wing versions of history that are now finding their way into our textbooks? Can subjectivity find a place in history?

I do not have a definitive answer for you. But I can offer an analogy:

Heisenberg's uncertainty principle. It states that we cannot simultaneously know both the exact position and the momentum of an electron because the photon used to 'see' the electron disturbs its position when it bounces off it, making the precise measurement of both variables impossible.

Of course, the macroworld and the nanoworld operate under different laws. But the idea that the very act of looking can change the reality that is being looked at is a valuable principle. Your position and perspective matters. Who you are—whether a Brahman, a Bengali, a Dalit, an Anglophile, a Communist or a left-leaning liberal—will shape what you *want* to believe. We can embody all these identities at once, or slip and slide from one to the other or prioritize one aspect over the other, and each will produce a different you with different values looking at the same historical situation.

If we don't start by implicating ourselves, the history we understand (and the history we teach) will be a history inflected by the old-fashioned and dangerously naive pretence that there can be a grand narrative, one that Bollywood has aspired to. A narrative with good guys and bad guys. And, at whose end, *Satyameva Jayate*, the truth shall prevail.

Let us take *Sholay*, for example. In the end, Thakur (Sanjeev Kumar), whose family has been destroyed by the bandit Gabbar Singh (Amjad Khan), pulls his foot back from Gabbar's head and does not crush him.

And here is the truth of the narrative of fiction. The original had Thakur killing Gabbar. The film was released around the Emergency, when violent films were supposed to be banned. But *Sholay* passed the censor, even though it was about vigilante justice and the failure of the state machinery. There are many reasons posited for this, including the friendship between Rajiv Gandhi and Amitabh Bachchan. One rumour is that the filmmakers were told to do the Gandhian thing—to have Thakur forgive at the end, for it to get passed. Which is the real ending? The one we all watched for years? The one we discovered after the arrival of the internet? The one we were used to and which we accepted as the moral conclusion; or the one written and filmed by the original creators?

Bollywood has constructed a cinema that reflects the world around us. And it is not an innocent reflection. It is a magic mirror that will let you see yourself the way you want to be seen. The image and the reflection are caught in a symbiotic relationship.

What is it you want to see?

What is it that you see?

BIOGRAPHY AS HISTORY

I will begin with a few thoughts on translation, mainly because such work as I have done in biography has largely been in the realm of translation. Perhaps the first was an autobiography of sorts: the actor Leela Naidu asked me whether I would help her write her life. When she told me the lineaments of it, I knew it would have to be a first-person account, because it would be difficult to check whether Louis Malle had really used her living room and all the carpets to create the right soundscape within which to record a classical performance in her home in J. A. Allana Marg, Mumbai; or to verify, as a good biographer should, where Jiddu Krishnamurthi was when he predicted that she would always see her children as if from behind glass. But to speak in her voice required more than an act of ventriloquism. It required me to take the acted—for Leela did not tell me stories so much as act them, so that she became the customs' officer or the Japanese photographer—and to turn facial expressions and certain telling gestures into words. It required me to set aside my gender, my age, my social history and inhabit the frail frame of a mature woman who had been declared one of the five most beautiful women in the world by *Vogue* magazine. I knew I had done a fair job when her long-time friend, Sunil Sethi, reviewed *Leela: A Patchwork Life* and said, 'Although written with the Mumbai journalist Jerry Pinto, who acted as amanuensis during her last withdrawn years in a Colaba flat, her voice rings funny, original and true.'[3]

The other biographies I have worked on are as a translator. I always think of a translator as someone who is rowing a boat made of salt across the river. Your boat is dissolving around you as you take it across, but you still try, because on the other side the need for salt is acute. Why? It differs from book to book, but, in India, the translator works at joining up the linguistic islands of the nation. She—and it is generally a woman—is building bridges across which meaning can pass. Perhaps I should make the second analogy clearer. The islands are low-lying, and the sea between them recedes often to allow some traffic. Thus in any major city, it is possible to encounter several languages at once. I get up in the morning and speak English to myself; then call an old aunt and speak in a mixture of Konkani, Portuguese and English; then I talk to the cab driver in Hindi; and then to an author I am translating, in Marathi; then a Parsi friend calls and, in ludic mode, I ask him, '*Kemchho, majjaamaa?*'

I know that each time I step out of English I am risking something—speaking to a senior woman in the tone meant for a junior, changing the gender of some inanimate object . . . I transgress in many languages, English included, but my transgressions are forgiven because most of my linguistic transactions are agenda-based. People want to know what I mean, so they will work at understanding my meaning. I will do the same when someone says something to me in a language I know a little better than he. This is how language works when it is not politicized. For all our romanticizing of it, language is also a tool. The story of language in India is the story of a great exchange, a grand migration, unabashed borrowings and re-usings on one side; and of equally strenuous attempts at purification and cleansing on the other.

My first translation was a book called *Cobalt Blue*, written by Sachin Kundalkar, a Brahman author.[4] I mention this because there is some cause to believe that being Brahman gives you a position of some legitimacy, some centrality. But if you are a gay Brahman boy in Pune, you are going to be an outsider not only in your community but also in many others. Thus, we must beware the seductions of easy categorization when dealing with how biography may impact a person's history. Kundalkar wrote this book when he was young; I have heard it said that he was in his twenties. The narrative is divided into two parts: Tanay tells the story of his love affair with their new Bohemian boarder; in the second half, Anuja, Tanay's sister, tells the story of her love affair with the same man. These simultaneous equations consist of two parts, hermetically sealed off from each other by the hypocrisy of the middle-class Maharashtrian family. (This can be read as any middle-class Indian family, but the narrative specificities are Maharashtrian, more specifically Punekari, though the city around has an imaginative geography comprising elements of Pune and Mumbai.) The son of the family is allowed to go upstairs and stay all night in the man's room but the girl, the sister, is not. So, she meets him outside. Since brother and sister never talk to each other about their sexuality, since there is a huge silence around matters of the heart, neither Tanay nor Anuja confide in each other, and this silence remains even at the end of the book. This was the silence that drew me into the book. It is the silence we have constructed for ourselves, a shelter against the things we do not want to hear. This is the great silence that haunts India. It is the silence that protects the paedophile, since children have no language, no words with which to talk to their parents about their bodies and their genitals. It is the silence that shrouds rape; survivors often say that it is tantamount to being violated again to go to a police station to recount what has happened, then to repeat it in court. Combine that with the family's fear of loss of honour and you can see why rape is under-reported. Then there is the silence that has descended on our media when fear brings self-censorship in its wake.

But let me backtrack from *Cobalt Blue* to the time my friend Naresh Fernandes and I put together an anthology called *Bombay, Meri Jaan: Writings on Mumbai.*[5] We wanted it to be as representative as possible to reflect

the nature of the city. Many of the
writers came from privilege, from the
middle-class, some were Dead White
European Men. We wanted voices from
the margins and although we had some
of Narayan Surve's poetry in an essay on
the mills, some of Namdeo Dhasal's as
well, we were deeply aware of how the
anthology needed more variety. But then,
I remembered that wonderful anthology
*Poisoned Bread: Translations from
Modern Marathi Dalit Literature* (Orient
Longman, 1992) edited by Arjun
Dangle.[6] I turned to it now and found an
excerpt called 'Son, Eat Your Fill' by
Daya Pawar, taken from his celebrated
autobiography, *Baluta*,[7] certainly the first
Marathi Dalit autobiography ever
written. It is a warm and wonderful
portrait of his grandmother, her

memories of the city, of the horse-drawn trams, of her working at a vet's clinic and of her sitting by his side as he ate, encouraging him to eat his fill. We used this excerpt in *Bombay Meri Jaan*.

Some years later, I was looking through the anthology and realized that I had not read *Baluta*, which is a classic. I knew that a French translation had come out, because Adil Jussawalla mentions it in an essay on Daya Pawar.[8] I was sure there would be an English translation as well, and, since reading in English is easier for me, I thought I should get hold of it. So, I asked Shanta Gokhale, my friend, the polymath and repository of knowledge of all things Marathi, whether it had been translated. She said it hadn't, and, without even thinking of the consequences, without even having read the book, I asked her if she thought I might make a good translator for it. Bless Shanta's heart, she said, 'Yes.' And I was launched as a translator.

I think there may be a lesson in there for all of us who call ourselves teachers. Often, when a student steps forward and asks, 'Do you think I can I do this?' we tend to respond with a tone of disbelief. '*You?*' we say because we remember every mistake s/he/they made, every disappointment to which we have been subjected. We are also perhaps trying to protect them from failure. My lesson as a teacher was that the more you trust a student, the more a student can trust herself.

*Baluta* was an important book, almost immediately recognized as a classic in the literary history of our country. At the beginning, Daya Pawar splits himself in two, and the two halves have a conversation. One half encourages the other to write; the other demurs, wondering who might want to read his book, asking whether his life might seem like a walking freak show of horrors. I was puzzling over why he was doing this and then I suddenly realized: What if you have never seen yourself in a book, what if there is no representation of your kind? What if you have been told repeatedly that your story has no significance? Name me the Dalit figures a teacher mentions in class? Dr Ambedkar? Mahatma Phule? Periyar? Jogendranath Mandal? Four, five, eight, maybe?—but it ends there. There are 200 million people out there and we represent them in our educational system with four or five names, condensed into an equal number of paragraphs! How do you think that feels? How do you think Daya Pawar felt when he finished his BA without hearing a word about Chokhamela, one of the greatest of Marathi saints? Chokhamela is canonical in Marathi saint literature but he gets little mention in Marathi textbooks. Therefore, in *Baluta*'s opening chapter, Pawar must encourage himself, because there's no one else to do so. There's no lineage, no history, no models and no references. But within twenty pages, he's hit his stride. His story has taken shape and he abandons those two halves. Now, there's just one Daya Pawar who is telling his story, who knows what he is doing. I trailed behind him, but then somewhere in the middle, he comes up with poetry, and I thought, 'Oh, I have to translate poetry now!' I believe there are two mountains in translation: one is humour and the other poetry. The first is a mountain because, though we all laugh, we laugh at different things, and while comedy can work magnificently without words, language immediately pins the comic down into a culture, a milieu, a philosophy, a music. The second is a mountain because a poem that is just words is not a poem. You can get the metre right, you can find a new rhythm that somewhat echoes the original one, you can get the words in the right order, but the spirit of the poem might elude you entirely. If you do not believe me, as an exercise, think of your favourite film song and then try translating it. You will see how banal it can become.

*Baluta* also made me aware of how my reading in Marathi had been a savarna Marathi. There is a point at which Pawar warns his readers that they might not have the vocabulary to cope with his book.

'The animal was divided according to the *gudsa*. This word appears in Laxmibai Tilak's autobiography. Who knows whether the Marathi litterateurs have heard of it or not? Laxmibai had heard of it. After all, she knew some Mahar Christians. Unless you know something about that caste, you wouldn't know.'

That there were many Marathis, I knew, because I have ears, and the variants of Marathi you hear in Mumbai have so many different and individual musics. Here was another way to look at language: through the prism of caste. If John Ruskin said that when he wanted to learn about a subject, he wrote a book on it, it seems to me an equally good way to learn about something by translating a book about it. So, I was delighted when I heard that the first volume of a dictionary of Dalit Marathi had come out. I bought it from a government printing press outlet. Of course, all the words I wanted to look up started with letters that did not appear in this volume. The next volume has not yet shown up.

*

On 14 April 1944, a ship comes into Bombay harbour, carrying cotton, explosives and gold with which to pay the troops. It is wartime, the ship is carrying various inflammable fluids, some of which have leaked. Cotton also catches fire easily, and suddenly the *SS Stikine* explodes. Four thousand tonnes of ship fly into the air and fall over other ships. Many Bombayites believe that the Japanese are attacking. Meanwhile, gold bricks fly through the air and crash into a Parsi gentleman's balcony.

The great thing about history is that it's always unbelievable and always weird—because it's made by human beings doing their thing. So, the Parsi gets up in the morning, finds the gold bricks and hands them over to the police. He is given an award, but refuses the money, directing it be given to help those who lost their lives or property to the Bombay Docks explosion.

Now, in *Baluta*, when this explosion takes place, all of Bombay is running *away* from the docks, which burned for several days. But the Mahars—Daya Pawar's people—are running *towards* the docks, because where there will be damage, there will be rubble, and where there is rubble, there is something to salvage and sell.

I read *Mee Mithaachi Baahuli* by Vandana Mishra (née Sushila Lotlikar), who wrote her autobiography when she was eighty-five.[9] Again, she is Brahman; again, her status is in question, not just because she is a woman (my friend, the classical musician Neela Bhagwat says that women are the *adi-dalit*, the first Dalits). Sushila Lotlikar was two years old when her father died of pneumonia, and her mother became the head of the family, training as a midwife because it was a short course and she would then be able to earn a living and support her family. Sushila is twelve when someone throws acid on her mother, leaving her bed-ridden. Now the girl must go to work, and she becomes an actress. She is a Maharashtrian girl who speaks Konkani at home, but her first job is on the Gujarati stage. She will act on the Gujarati stage for years, and become a bit of a star but will get only second leads. She will break out and become a Marwari theatre star. Then, at the height of her career, her mother will tell her that she should get married—so she does, at twenty-one, and retires from the stage, settles down and has three children.

Sushila too has a story about the Bombay dock explosion: She's on stage, and the audience hears the blast; small wonder, the seismographs in Shimla recorded it. She writes:

> When the explosion took place in the docks, I was acting in a Gujarati play at the Bhangwadi Theatre. We felt a huge thump. We had no idea what had happened. The audience was terrified and the show had to be brought to an end rapidly. Qasimbhai, the producer, sent someone to accompany me home. All down the road, there were clouds of smoke and a feeling of terror. It was only when I got home that Aai relaxed. 'Gosh, Babi, the vessels I had placed on the shelf fell off on their own. I don't know what's going on,' she said.

But the following day, as the city burns and people are fighting the flames, she is back on stage again.

It did not seem odd then, that even while one area of the city had been levelled, the next day five thousand Marathi people should come to Chowpatty to see a play. But today, this does seem extraordinary.

Same event, two prisms. What is your prism like?

This is what biography can teach history. The Greek philosopher Heraclitus taught us that you can never cross the same river twice. But you can have several river crossings—a metaphor which carries much weight in India—in fact, as many river crossings as there are observers.

Take the case of *Mala Uddhvasta Vhaychay* by Malika Amar Sheikh, which I translated into English as *I Want to Destroy Myself.*[10] Malika Amar Sheikh had a ringside view of history. Her father was the noted revolutionary poet Amar Sheikh, who died young in an 'accident'. Her husband was the noted revolutionary poet Namdeo Dhasal, who also founded the Dalit Panthers, a movement based on the Black Panthers of America. She tells her story with great honesty and a complete lack of guile. She speaks of the tragedy of losing her father, the abuse she suffered at the hands of her husband and the breakdown of her marriage. For many readers, this was a new perspective on events. Namdeo Dhasal was the poet who had blown Marathi literary sensibility out of the water—now he was also the man who had mistreated his wife. The book offers a female prism with which to view Namdeo Dhasal, very much a man's man, a male poet living in a male world. As my friend, the writer and activist Urmila Pawar points out, the patriarchy operates differently in the margins of society but its operations are still recognizable and must still be countered. Women telling their stories provide a much-needed corrective.

Eknath Awad's book *Jag Badal Ghaluni Ghav*[11] was brought to my attention by his son, Professor Milind Awad. It is an extraordinary story. Most Dalits follow Dr Babasaheb Ambedkar's advice to leave the village and come to the city. Eknath Awad arrives in the city, gets a job and begins to work with an

NGO but feels he must go back to the village because the real caste wars are fought there. Most of these struggles are non-violent; Mr Awad borrows from the ahimsa playbook, but he is not above wielding a bamboo and urging others to do so. He tells us a secret: that it is not enough for a law to be passed, it must be turned into action and that action begins when the legislature reaches out to the bureaucracy and the bureaucracy unlocks this and lets the public know.

I think it might be useful for each of us to think of what we know about history as a quilt. We have stitched together a portrait of a person or a time or an event from a number of sources. We may think our quilt as particularly fine but if it is examined from another perspective, one that is not yours, it might be found to be a little threadbare. How does our quilt measure up when someone asks: how many women figure in this story, how did you demonstrate that their lives mattered? How does your quilt look when someone begins to question how many Dalit lives are mentioned? How does your quilt stand up to the question of where the aboriginal, the tribal, the farmer, fits in? Is your quilt rich with kings and princes and emperors and presidents and prime ministers and foreign ministers? How would your quilt stand up if the North Eastern woman went looking for the names of her people in it? Do the names of Henry Kissinger and Bismarck mean more than the names of Birsa Munda and Imliakum Ao? This is where translation faces such immense challenges that I sometimes feel a deeply personal sense of despair about how little meaningful progress we seem to be making.

To me, history is a story. Etymologically, it is *histoire*, the story. A pun might render it as his-story, the story of the upper-class privileged male. This story has no place for fiction, we are told. I think that's not a particularly useful distinction, because fiction often offers the reader clues to the thoughts and feelings and worldviews of its characters. Yes, these tend to be middle-class people because middle-class men and women generally write fiction, but we should know by now that we are all required to look more carefully at identity politics.

Through fiction, we are looking at how people look at others and how they look at themselves. So, *Cobalt Blue* is an answer to many RSS claims that homosexuality is a Western phenomenon, that it didn't exist in India. Is this of any relevance to us as teachers? Do we mention the sexuality of a historical figure? Or do we just allow our students to assume that the world is a heteronormative parade? There might be a student in class who is wondering: am I the only one who feels this way?

There is a horrible silence around many things, around being born in the wrong body, around being gay, around being Dalit, around being Muslim. A teacher can break the silence, and a teacher can break it ex-cathedra.

When I walk into a classroom, I begin by telling my postgraduate students, 'This is going to be no holds barred.' It is a media class, the majority of the students are women. I make it clear: 'We will obviously be talking about sexuality. If you feel uncomfortable at any point, you need to be able to openly say, "I don't want you to be talking about that."' So far, very few students have raised red flags, but I believe we must let them know at the beginning that it is their right to do so. Now that the space has been opened, we discuss issues like female genital mutilation and male rape, among the many other topics that emerge in the news. The media bring terrible realities to light every day and these make their way into my class.

Over the last twenty-five years, I have resisted the temptation of a 'one size fits all' theory for teaching. This generally goes by the name of a syllabus. My class is a living, breathing entity, and I must try to be completely responsive to it— connecting through silence or through speech as needed. Both forms of communication deserve respect. Too often, students are denied agency in classrooms, conditioned to defer to teachers and texts. They resent this lack of agency yet also fear it, having spent years in an education system that rewards conformity and punishes deviation.

They must discover the silences. When we look at the history of the Indian Independence movement, I ask students to analyse their textbooks: How many women are mentioned? How are they represented? When students discover these disparities themselves, it has a far greater impact than if I were to simply tell them, 'Women have been silenced.'

What qualities do we attribute to silence, and what do we attribute to speech? Silence can fester, just as speech can explode. Is our silence in the face of an atrocity golden? On the other hand, speech, while powerful, can also be disruptive and we have felt the need for laws to protect ourselves from the voices of untruth.

But how do we speak for others? How can I write about women or Dalits if my life has been one of privilege? One of the greatest tools we have is self-implication. Self-implication demands that I explicitly acknowledge my position as a Roman Catholic middle-class male before I say anything about the marginalized. We cannot erase our identities, nor should we attempt to. Instead, we must bridge gaps until the day comes when marginal voices can represent themselves without the mediation of others. Utopia, however, will always be postponed. Every moment in literary history is fraught and incomplete, a reflection of human imperfection. The key lies in archaeology and excavation. Our task is to document marginal narratives before they are lost, much like the Brothers Grimm documented folk tales.

And even when we discuss the marginalized, what do we highlight? For example, we could say that Dr Babasaheb Ambedkar headed the Constituent Assembly, that he was a Dalit, a Maharashtrian, or that he was educated at Columbia University. Each one presents a point of view, each one is a prism. By highlighting one over the other, you have not departed from historic fact—but you have set an agenda. Self-implication requires you to ask yourself what your agenda is in your selection of the facts.

*

Allow me a small digression. My novel *Em and the Big Hoom* tells the story of the Mendes family. Em, the mother, suffers from bipolar disorder.[12] She is based on my mother who suffered the same illness. I tried to write my account of our situation as nonfiction but it did not work. I turned it into a novel because I needed some distance. At public readings to promote the book, people would often narrate their experiences. When raw emotion is let loose in a room, you have to be trained to deal with it. I told a friend about my unease with this situation and she said, 'Tell them to write.' This might be one way to try and make something out of the pain, to take the pain somewhere. So, I started telling people to write, and then one of them actually did and sent the piece to me. I began to think about this as the seed of a book. This is another function of the story, of history: the story makes other stories happen, a history is the catalyst for other histories.

Most of the people who wrote for *A Book of Light: When a Loved One Has a Different Mind* were caregivers,[13] people who lived with the person suffering the affliction. The last one was Nirupama Dutt, who wrote about her daughter, a special-needs person, has recently become a mother herself. Dutt told me of a young man who wanted to write about his father, the playwright Swadesh Deepak. I had seen his drama, *Court Martial*, set in the Indian Army.[14] Apparently, after he wrote this play, Swadesh Deepak had what is called a nervous breakdown. He tried to kill himself—he slashed his wrists, then set himself on fire and was burnt so severely that at AIIMS, Chandigarh, they could not decide whether to admit him to the burns unit or the psychiatric unit. After seven years of this, he began to heal. Once he had recovered, his friends urged him to write about his experiences. And he did: *Maine Mandu Nahi Dekha* (I have not seen Mandu).[15]

If you grew up with a mother who had mental health issues, you might find yourself reading constantly about mental health—devouring anything you can get your hands on. You want to understand, to decode what's happening, to find something magical, a talisman, or a guide to the world. I, who had read so much had somehow missed this book!? So, I began reading it, and, truly, I had never encountered anything like it. It stood out not just because mental health narratives are rare in India, but also because it is a formally stunning book. Deepak calls it a *khandit* collage—a fractured collage and there are many times in which you see the cracks and the breaks. Time is fluid and we travel back and forth. The real and the imaginary segue into each other: Deepak is visited by the shade of Yeats who has learned Hindi to talk to Nirala on the other side. Characters from his own fiction visit him.

But the book itself begins with a vivid description of dinner at the house of Nirmal Verma and Gagan Gill. Suddenly, I was a fly on the wall in Nirmal Verma's house as Krishna Sobti and others are bantering before dinner.

Then the narrative begins to darken. As you read, it becomes clear that the author is still not very well. Deepak walks on thin ice through the whole of the book. Two years after its release, he disappeared. One morning in 2006, he walked out of his house and never returned. We still don't know where he is.

History is often seen in terms of a grand narrative, but what it really boils down to is: what happened to people? And you cannot understand that unless you know how the people lived. To know that you construct a norm. This norm becomes the subject of history. A massive synecdoche is created, a part for the whole, and the part is an illusion, a composite picture. Does this composite picture ever represent Imelda Mendes? Or Swadesh Deepak? Does this picture represent Eknath Awad, Daya Pawar or Mallika Amar Sheikh?

How do we represent the family? How do we look at the family in the world? How does a family live in a world where mental health is seen as a luxury only the monied can afford? What is history if it only represents an illusion?

So what am I saying? I am saying: read fiction next to nonfiction. Read biographies and autobiographies to see how history is shaped by people and people shaped by history. We have so much more access now. It is time to use it.

# MOTHERS AND OTHERS

### HOW TO BRING THE MARGINS
### BACK INTO YOUNG LIVES

I did not want to become a teacher. I became one at the age of fourteen out of the usual adolescent compulsions. At that point in time, I needed money for what I saw as the creature comforts of life. I was not interested in the philosophy of education or the power structures underlying teaching. I understood these in the pragmatic way that an intelligent fourteen-year-old does, from the experience of their inequities and inequalities. I would spend the next decade in educational institutions on the wrong side of the equation, the powerless side, and then segue effortlessly to the powerful side of the equation when I went out to teach. My students did not care much for what they were learning or even why. I saw in most of their faces the stoicism of the animal attached to the Persian wheel. Someone, somewhere had decreed that we should take their animal energy and tame it and set it down on a bench. Meanwhile, we, a taskforce of teachers, would force-feed them facts and methods. As a tutor, I was an additional imposition, a further restriction on free time, play time, dream time, lounge time, laze time and all the things children would want to do. And so, my students did not want to be excited or enthused. They wanted to be freed. They wanted to get past exams. They wanted marks. I was therefore tasked to teach them how to do things to get those marks: how to solve a quadratic equation, how to recognize an adverb clause of condition. I was an enabler for a bad system.

The only thing I can say to my credit for the first dozen years or so of my life as a teacher was that I was the only tutor I knew who accepted students who were doing badly. Most other mathematics tutors wanted students who were doing well; they were looking to help students turn their 88s into 98s. This seemed patently ridiculous from the outside; but if you look at it from the perspective of the tutor, he (and it was generally a male) was protecting his market. If he had students who did not score 90s, he would not get more students the following year. And the only way to make sure that your students get 90s is to take students who are getting 80s.

If you think this is stupid, go and ask a school principal whether s/he takes students who need education or students who are already in a position to be educated. Find out whether schools prefer to take in first-generation learners or would rather admit those whose parents are both postgraduates. Ask whether the school wants to help children who don't know any English or would prefer to have students who already speak English when they are admitted. If the latter, then please don't laugh at the tutors of mathematics in the city of Mumbai; they are only reflections of the system. Every educational institution is the same; they choose the best and then pride themselves on excellent results. I took the worst and I was proud when they began to relax enough to get mathematics, and I was delighted when they scored marks in the 60s. I was known as 'Duffer Sir' and I was proud of the label.

The reason why I could help students who were flailing was because I had once been there. But then came a moment in my life, a moment of transition. I was sitting in math class when Mrs Lidwin D'Souza walked past my desk. I hunched over my work in the same protective manner that poor students use when their teachers hove to. She stopped and said, 'Jerry, do you understand English?'

I said I did.

'Do you have a logical mind?'

I said I thought I did.

'Then logic plus language is mathematics. Mathematics is a language. Mathematics is a language, if you are good at language, you should be good at maths.'

I had always thought that mathematics was a handmaid of science.

So the next time I saw her I asked how it was a language. She said, '2 is a number, plus is a verb, 2 plus 2 equals 4 is a sentence. It is just a precise language.'

Suddenly, instead of drowning in mathematics, I was floating on top of it.

I wish I could say that I saw there the magic of teaching, that you could take a child and with a simple analogy reconstruct the world of learning for her or him.

This did happen to me but I did not recognize this magic nor did I seek to be a mage. I wanted instead to make money.

And I made a lot of money. I started at the age of fifteen and stopped at the age of thirty because I had become extremely good at it. This may seem like a conundrum or a pretty Chestertonianism but you can get burnt out. I had.

This did not mean I had stopped teaching.

At about the age of twenty-five, the Social Communications Media Department of the Sophia Polytechnic made a signal mistake. The gentleman who ran the journalism practicals was on leave, and a young woman I knew from my time as a freelance journalist at the *Free Press Journal*, Kaumudi Marathe, recommended my name. I had been writing for about five years then and didn't think anyone would take me seriously, but when the head of department, the redoubtable Jeroo Mulla called, I went in for an interview, because the college was close to the areas where I had my mathematics students. I was interviewed in about three minutes and given the job. They must have been desperate or disinterested.

It was only then that it occurred to me that I did not know what I should be doing in that class for the rest of the year. I had never been taught journalism, so I had no models to fall back on. In retrospect, that might have even been a good thing, because I invented it as I went along. Until the time I took over, the students seemed to have a cushy time

in their journalism practicals. They
interviewed each other, set up mock press
conferences . . . they played at
journalism.

I thought that the only way to teach
them what it was really like was to send
them out into the field. Many of them
were from city cocoons. They lived in the
posh areas of the city and had hardly
ever talked to strangers. In the first few
years, I conceived the idea of the City
Beats. This involved pairing a student
with a suburb she had never heard of and
making her visit it regularly for the rest
of the year, to generate a series of stories
from that space. It was my first attempt
at decentring their lives. They were all
Anglophone elites then, but they quickly
discovered that they could speak other
languages, other Indian languages, other

*bhashas*, when they needed to go to a police station or the municipal office. Every year, the beats are greeted with horror. At the end of every year, they are remembered with the nostalgia and affection the young reserve for a rite of passage.

Half of our students come from outside the city. In the first week, I would tell the entire class that they would have to go and interview a celebrity.

The class would squeak in outrage. 'I don't know any celebrities.' 'I've just landed from Chennai and I don't know *anyone*.'

To which my answer would be: 'Too bad, you're going to fail journalism.' I know. I shouldn't do that but at that stage, they are still students and the Pavlovian response of fifteen years of indoctrination is hard to break and easy to use. Every year, the young woman from Chennai, the quiet young woman from Jorhat, all of them go out into the city and come back with a celebrity interview. One person sat outside Lata Mangeshkar's house for eight hours. We talk to our students about persistence, but as teachers we rarely practise it ourselves. You can be taught by a student and that student taught me a lesson. I often asked myself whether I was feeding into the celebrity culture that we so decry. But I needed a way to show my students that they could climb any mountain I slammed down in front of them. The gains in self-confidence were well worth it.

I started by pushing them and found that each time I pushed them they pushed back magically. But these were postgraduate students who had come through a system that is only interested in the analytical, the metaphoric, the symbolic logic of language and interpretation. They were all bright students who lived in their left brains, the analytical side of their heads. (Yes, I am aware that this is a theory that has been disproved, but let me use it here for the purposes of this argument.) These were students who were happiest when they had something to think about. So I tried to think of ways in which we could get the body involved. And I hit upon the idea of performance. Was this journalism? By this time, five or six years into teaching, I didn't really care. I wanted to shake my class up. I wanted the ones whose language was the language of the body, who jumped up to dance, those students, I wanted them to be front and centre. And I wanted to break the Anglophone grip on our thoughts. The students were already divided into teams; I would assign one team the task of writing and singing and dancing a laavni on Freud; the second would perform a bhavai on Marx; the third would do a qawwali on Einstein. First would come the research on the subject. Then the writing of the lyrics, the working out of the script, composing the music, choreographing the dance, blocking the movements, rehearsals, finally: performance.

I enjoyed watching the top five of the class struggle with this. These are the students who are quite used to excelling in class because they have the right kind of brain for our systems: they excel in reading and writing, but dancing? You could see them counting down the minutes. You could see how difficult it was to accept that a classmate—the one who never seems to know the answers when someone asks questions about Chomsky—that person is now choreographing everyone and finding them wanting, settling them in the back.

Students are tribal in nature. They hang together in groups. These groups are built on similarities: do we speak the same kind of English, do we have the same experiences, do we share a demographic? It is unconscious and it is unconscionable. I wanted to shake my top five out of their stupor. The world is large and it does not have a fixed syllabus. You had better learn to make

space for other kinds of skills,
acknowledge other kinds of talents.
Learning happens when you step outside
the tribalism.

It is wise, I have discovered, not to
romanticize your students, they are as
disgusting as we are. But if we both
acknowledge that we are works in
progress, if we can find a place to share
what we are and what we want to be, we
can make a different kind of magic.

*

One of my classes would begin with me
reading out this passage:

> Because woman's work is never
> done and is underpaid or unpaid
> or boring or repetitious and we're
> the first to get fired and what we

look like is more important than
what we do and if we get raped
it's our fault and if we get beaten
we must have provoked it and if
we raise our voices we're nagging
bitches and if we enjoy sex we're
nymphos and if we don't we're
frigid and if we love women it's
because we can't get a 'real' man
and if we ask our doctor too
many questions we're neurotic
and/or pushy and if we expect
childcare we're selfish and if we
stand up for our rights we're
aggressive and 'unfeminine' and if
we don't we're typical weak
females and if we want to get
married we're out to trap a man
and if we don't we're unnatural
and because we still can't get an
adequate safe contraceptive but

men can walk on the moon and if
we can't cope or don't want a
pregnancy we're made to feel
guilty about abortion and . . . for
lots and lots of other reasons we
are part of the women's liberation
movement.[16]

Then I would get them to read it out,
aloud, and then I would ask them to
chant it and finally to scream it. Then
they would have to translate it into their
mother tongues and write it on postcards
for their grandmothers and grandaunts.

The responses were interesting. Some
of the senior women were appalled. Some
were amused and others were deeply
moved. An old Punjabi lady told her
granddaughter that she was glad someone
had said what she had been thinking for
so many years.

In class, we often talked about the erasure of women. *Em and the Big Hoom* is about my mother who was erased from our family's public sphere because she was mentally ill or neurodivergent. People talked about her as she had been; they were afraid to address her reality in the present. I think, in some ways, this novel was my way of saying: I do not remember the beautiful young woman who sang in the Paranjoti Choir and who worked at the American Consulate. I remember this woman, walking around barefoot, unwashed, smoking and garrulous, refusing to play any role that were assigned to married women. This is the woman I love.

Perhaps much of my writing career was about reinstating women who had, in some way or the other, slipped out of the public eye. I could see Leela Naidu being erased or subsumed in her role as Dom Moraes's wife, so I helped her write her autobiography: *Leela: A Patchwork Life*.

I could see that Helen was a dancer who defied the patriarchy. In general, male stars are granted long screen lives. An Amitabh Bachchan will play Raakhee Gulzar's younger brother in *Reshma aur Shera* (directed by Sunil Dutt) in 1971, her lover in the 1978 release *Muqaddar Ka Sikandar* (directed by Prakash Mehra) and in the 1979 release *Jurmana* (directed by Hrishikesh Mukherjee) and in *Bemisal* (Hrishikesh Mukherkjee, 1982) and then her son in *Shakti* (directed by Ramesh Sippy) which came out in the same year. Helen vamped three generations of Hindi film stars: Prithviraj

Kapoor (in B. K. Adarsh's *Harishchandra Taramati*, 1963) Raj Kapoor (in Hrishikesh Mukherjee's *Anari*, 1959) and Rishi Kapoor (in Sikandar Khanna's *Phool Khile Hain Gulshan Gulshan*, 1978), and yet the only thing anyone could find to say about her was that she was the 'original item girl'. In writing about her, I wanted to point out that a marginal figure had to teach us about the moral universe we had invented in Bollywood.

Even in the translations that I do, there have been some retrieval acts, Malika Amar Sheikh's *I Want to Destroy Myself* was a classic work, and Vandana Mishra's *I, the Salt Doll* was another. The Anglophone reader in India and across the world should have access to these books, so different in their world views and so different in their attitudes to Bombay and the world of work. But how might we turn into action all our talk about the erasure of women from the histories of our world?

'How much do you know about your mother?' I asked my class. They were all quite sure they knew their mothers well. 'That's great, because now you have to write 5,000 words on her.' This is the final step in a pedagogy of numbers. My class begins with 500-word pieces; they move on to 1000-word pieces; then 1,500. And this is the final summit they must scale. (Why am I so numerically obsessive? Because the field of journalism to which they are headed is numerically obsessed. For in a polytechnic course, we must keep one eye firmly fixed on industry and its demands. I am not one of those who believes in 'skills' on their own; skills without values are dangerous; and values without history are impossible.)

In the first set that I received, I saw the way the students would fill up the pages with the senseless emotionalism of greeting cards. And so I put a ban on all regurgitations of the notion of 'Mother'. What struck me was how few facts there were. I am amazed at how many mothers were born on 1 January. Then I discovered that those were Dalit mothers. Their parents could not remember their date of birth. And so when the child is admitted to school or to some other programme and the date of birth is demanded of the parents, they generally explain the year, 'the year of the flood', 'the year after the locust attack' and then

the officer would use 1 January as a
default setting. Otherwise, it would be 26
January or 15 August. These are the three
dates on which many Dalits are born.
And so we had to look for facts and
understand what had become the facts.
The date of her birth. Her name before
marriage (if it had been changed). Her
education, school, college. Whatever data
they could gather was valuable, I
thought, because it added something to
our knowledge of women of twenty,
thirty years ago. And then there was the
other question: who was your mother
before she became a mother? (This is
because I believe a child is a machine to
make a woman a second-class citizen in
her own life. But it is so beautifully
designed that when she becomes a
mother, she voluntarily gives up first-class

citizenship.) Did she have a boyfriend? Was she peeled away from that boyfriend to be married to your father? Did she have a 'best friend' in school? Did she go to college? Was it the college of her choice? Did she study the subjects of her choice or were those dictated by her parents?

Sometimes a student would come up to me and say, 'I think my mother is inventing things. She talks about her home as if it were a palace and I've been there and it's nothing like she remembers it.' My response: 'It might have been a palace from the point of view of an exile. It might have been a palace in which she was loved for who she was. It might have been a palace because she loved it. Now set down her description and set down next to it your description of it.'

Gitanjali (name changed) told me a terrifying story which she heard from her mother's elder sister, Sandhya. Sandhya was one of several daughters. She was fifteen when Gitanjali's mother was born. One day, she walked into her mother's room and found her trying to drown her newest born in a bucket of milk. Sandhya saw what was happening and grabbed the baby, pulled it out and became a surrogate mother to the infant. She would only bring her youngest sister to her mother to be fed. My student confronted her grandmother about the story. Her grandmother said that she had been misunderstood. She had been washing the baby in milk so as to improve her complexion. When my student told me this, she was in a wash of tears. But this began a process by which she understood why her Sandhya maasi was so important in her mother's life, and a healing process began in that relationship.

The next step is to divide the class into three teams, each selecting a woman who has been overlooked by history and to collaborate on writing a 10,000-word essay about her. The result: *Lives of the Women*, a series of books.[17] There are days when you think that students are only motivated by marks. And then there are times when you and your students accomplish something like this without any grading involved. We have produced three volumes in five years. The students did them simply to say that these women—Shanta Gokhale, Dolly Thakore, Meera Devidayal, Shama Habibullah, Rekha Sabnis, among others—are important.

*

I remember talking to the department about how we have very few students from the Dalit and Muslim communities—they disagreed, saying that they do offer scholarships for these communities. But which underprivileged student would choose to apply to Sophia Polytechnic when they can see that a course costs lakhs of rupees? So we began to reach out to underprivileged communities themselves.

Three years ago, we had a very pleasant young woman who pleasantly refused to believe that caste was still an issue in the country, because she said that she didn't know anything about caste. (You know exactly where that is coming from. Since caste was not an issue for her, it could not be an issue for anybody.) Towards the end of the year, she struggled to find a topic for *Marginalia*, a magazine focusing on marginalized voices. I suggested she write about the Brihanmumbai Municipal Corporation (BMC) conservancy worker—a suggestion I often make, because I want my students to witness what happens to the sanitary napkins after they are thrown away.

So this young woman took up the story and shadowed a BMC worker. He took her into lanes brimming with filth, dead rats floating in the gutters he had to clean, garbage being thrown from windows. When she returned, she admitted she now understood the harsh realities of caste. As part of her story, she visited his home, where she was invited to share a meal with his family, and even though her parents objected, she chose to go.

At that dinner, the worker's younger son accused her of engaging in poverty tourism: he said that she had come to 'look' at them and to use them to succeed. They would remain where they were but their story would be this young woman's route to success. She was hurt, but she said, 'I'm sorry you feel that way. Tell me about yourself.' This was disarming—it meant she had some interest in him as a person, and not merely as character in her story. He said that he wanted to become a photojournalist and that he could not afford applying to the programme she was in. She promised him a scholarship. 'He is applying next year. You must find a way to get him in,' she told us.

The next year, he was in class.

*

You can never know what to expect. I record here a conversation between a student and me, at the beginning of the year.

'Don't mind, Sir, but you have given me this area to cover . . . I don't feel comfortable going there. Let's put it frankly, it is a Muslim area in Bombay.'

'Why don't you feel comfortable there?'

'I just don't.'

'As a media person, you will have to locate yourself, to implicate yourself in the story you are telling. For that you need self-awareness, you have to be able to deconstruct why you don't feel comfortable.'

The next day, my young student explained that in these areas, there are lots of people with funny looks.

'What does that mean: funny looks? Are they looking at you funnily or do they look funny?'

She said that all the men had beards and moustaches.

'Nobody in your family with a beard?'

'Not *that* kind of beard.'

'All right . . . I could excuse you and give you another beat. But just go to this place for three or four days in the evening and talk to a few different women and come back.'

A week later, she submitted her first piece from the area. By the second week, she'd written another. When we met, I asked if she still felt uncomfortable there. She smiled sheepishly and said, 'No, the women are so friendly. They show me around, they even suggest stories and help with them.'

She still maintains her ties with that neighbourhood. She's invited to weddings, joins them for iftar and continues to tell their stories.

You can cause change to happen one person at a time, but that will happen only when you recognize the basic humanity on the other side. She has short hair and wears a dress, but she still has the same problems as you, she is still probably going through menopause like you, she is still probably getting hot flushes like you, she probably has a mother-in-law just like yours, she probably had to give a dowry just like you did. There is just that superficial difference of where you put your caste marking, your bodily marking of how the husband claimed you—she probably put it on her left finger and you put it in the parting of your hair. (We mark the woman's body so that everyone will know that she is married, but we don't mark the man's body, though in all fairness, I have to say that Christian men wear wedding rings too.) We cannot expect the nation to transform into a magical wonderland of peace where everything is wonderful and happy, unless each one of us tries to be part of the solution. We are running out of time.

*

I was once sitting in a train in Bombay, eating dates, when a man sitting in front of me remarked, 'You don't look like a Muslim.'

I don't mind with being thought a Muslim—or anything else, for that matter—but I couldn't help but ask: 'Why do you think I'm a Muslim?'

'Because you're eating dates,' he said.

Dates are now associated with Muslims? I asked him if he believed in God.

He said he did.

I asked whether he believed that God had created the date palm.

He said that God had.

'Did God create the date palm for the Muslims?'

'No,' he said. 'There were dates before there was Islam.'

'Did God earmark the date palm for Muslims?'

He shook his head. 'No, God doesn't do that. Man does.'

'Well, if man does it, man can undo it,' I pointed out and offered him a date. He declined politely. He had just eaten, he said.

The man was a chartered accountant, he told me. He was an educated man, but he had internalized some strange ideas about fruit. These were probably not his ideas; they had come to him from the intellectual ecosystem in which he lived. It struck me then: He might have been a good student but the system had failed him because it had not taught him to think critically.

Whenever I say I translate from Marathi, the first question a sweet old lady will ask is, do you know enough Marathi? I recognize the communal tone of that question. It is only being asked because my name is Jerry Pinto and that sounds like the name of a Goan Roman Catholic. She would never ask this question if my name were Jayatirth Pant, because a Hindu name would imply that knowledge of Marathi would be automatic; this is not true for a Christian from Goa, specially since Bollywood has us down for the laughs when we open our mouths in the films. Without knowing it, she was othering me. Without meaning to, perhaps she was doubting my credentials. I was not, in her eyes, the obvious translator. I was not, in her eyes, the perfect translator. Who is the perfect translator? As part of the subset of requirements, where does my identity come in? How important is it in the larger scheme of things? My sweet old lady interlocutor has not been taught to ask herself the question: What does it mean to say that? What is at the base of my questioning?

We are not tasked with knowing the absolute truth; instead, we are asked to be part of a process by which we must introduce our students to the idea of how mutable truth is, how fragile and how it is shaped by the moment, by the people involved and their collective understanding. How much easier for all of us if we could deal with certainties. How often we retreat there. But we must learn that democracy, if it is to work, must be a series of negotiations. It will be slow and clumsy because of this; fascism is always in a hurry and its brutality lies in this rush to clean up, to tuck out of sight, to make everything look a certain way.

To teach from a position of uncertainty is not easy. But it is what we are asked to do. There's that old Chinese curse: May you live in interesting times. How much more interesting can they get?

## NOTES

1   Anuradha Kapur, 'Deity to Crusader: The Changing Iconography of Ram' in Gyanendra Pandey (ed.), *The Question of Identity in India Today* (New Delhi: Penguin, 1993).

2   I am indebted to the Australian writer Debra Dank for this observation.

3   Sunil Sethi, 'Wages of Whimsy', *Outlook* (15 June 2010).

4   Sachin Kundalkar, *Cobalt Blue* (Jerry Pinto trans.) (London: Hamish Hamilton, 2013).

5   Jerry Pinto and Naresh Fernandes (eds), *Bombay, Meri Jaan: Writings on Mumbai* (New Delhi: Penguin, 2018).

6   Arjun Dangle (ed.), Poisoned Bread:
    Translations from Modern Marathi Dalit
    Literature (Hyderabad: Orient Blackswan,
    1992).

7   Daya Pawar, *Baluta* (Mumbai: Granthali,
    1978).

8   Adil Jussawalla, 'With Daya Pawar in Paris' in
    *Maps for a Mortal Moon: Essays and
    Entertainments* (Jerry Pinto ed. and intro.)
    (New Delhi: Alpeh, 2014).

9   Vandana Mishra, *Mee Mithaachi Baahuli*
    (Pune: Rajhans Prakashan, 2014). Translated
    by Jerry Pinto as *I, the Salt Doll* (New Delhi:
    Speaking Tiger, 2016).

10  Malika Amar Sheikh, *Mala Uddhavast
    Vhayachay* (Kolhapur: Riya, 1994).
    Translated by Jerry Pinto as *I Want to
    Destroy Myself* (New Delhi: Speaking Tiger,
    2016).

11  Eknath Awad, *Jag Badal Ghaluni Ghav* (Pune:
    Samakaleen Prakashan, 2011). Translated by
    Jerry Pinto as *Strike a Blow to Change the
    World* (New Delhi: Speaking Tiger, 2018).

12  Jerry Pinto, *Em and the Big Hoom* (New

Delhi: Aleph, 2012).

13   Jerry Pinto, *A Book of Light: When a Loved One Has a Different Mind* (New Delhi: Speaking Tiger, 2016).

14   Swadesh Deepak, *Court Martial and Other Plays* (New Delhi: Speaking Tiger, 2024).

15   Swadesh Deepak, *Maine Mandu Nahi Dekha* (New Delhi: Vani Prakashan, 2003). Translated by Jerry Pinto as *I Have Not Seen Mandu* (New Delhi: Speaking Tiger, 2021).

16   Source unconfirmed; now proverbial. Probably authored by Joyce Stevens for a broadsheet published on International Women's Day, 1975.

17   The *Lives of the Women* series can be accessed here: scmsophia.com/books